C000181233

A
BIRDS OF PREY

by Carolyn Thomson and John Dell

DEPARTMENT OF CONSERVATION AND LAND MANAGEMENT

Birds of prey, or raptors, have long captured the imagination of people. These handsome creatures have a unique place in our culture and mythology. Birds of prey, which include hawks, falcons, kites, harriers, buzzards and eagles, are often symbols of power, vision, speed and audacity. Their majestic demeanour has been reflected in terms such as "to fly like an eagle". The word raptor is derived from the Latin word rapere, which means "to snatch".

These predatory birds are active during the day. Because of their need to spot slight movement of their prey, the ability to discern detail sharply may be as much as eight times keener in the larger birds of prey than in man. Female raptors are always larger than their male counterparts. There are 24 species of raptor in Australia, and all are found in WA. Three Western Australian species, the red goshawk, the grey falcon and the peregrine falcon, are rare and are officially listed as threatened species.

There are a variety of raptors with different characteristics. Hawks, for instance, typically have short rounded wings and a long tail. Kites usually have a long forked tail and long, broad wings, and typically prey on small mammals and insects. Harriers have broad wings, long legs and tails, and they prey on small terrestrial animals. Eagles are known for their large, broad wings and strong soaring flight. Falcons are placed in a different family to eagles, hawks, harriers and kites. They have pointed wings and a long tail. A Guide to Identification has been provided on pages 4-11 to help you distinguish between different birds of prey.

Above: *Nankeen kestrel*

Many birds of prey are often difficult to identify because they may be seen at a distance or as a mere silhouette. However, you can identify most if you carefully note particular features such as the shape of the tail (square, rounded or wedge-shaped) and its relative length (short or long), the angle and shape of the wings, the general size of the bird, and any distinctive colour patterns. Key identification features are shown in italics in the sections below.

OSPREYS

OSPREY - *Long narrow arched wings,* long narrow squarish tail, small head with small *crest.* Top of head white with dark patches. Distinctive *black band along side of head and neck.* Dark back, white underneath. Found along coasts and estuarine parts of rivers. Sits on exposed perches. Dives feet first into water to catch fish. **Pages 12-13.**

LARGE EAGLES

WHITE-BREASTED SEA-EAGLE - *Broad wings held high when soaring. Short wedge-shaped tail. White head, neck and underparts.* Grey back. *White tail with black band at base.* Juveniles are streaked brown and may be mistaken for young wedge-tailed eagles. Found along coasts and banks of rivers and inland lakes. **Pages 14-15.**

wedge-tailed eagle

WEDGE-TAILED EAGLE - *Broad wings held high when soaring. Long wedge-shaped tail. Adults blackish with pale beak.* Juveniles are various shades of brown. Found throughout Australia except in heavily forested areas. Often seen feeding on carcasses along roads. **Pages 16-17.**

MEDIUM-SIZED EAGLES AND KITES

Seven species, all with distinctive characteristics. Tail shape and size, wing pattern, shape, size, and angle when flying, flight methods and hunting are key identification techniques. All have deeply fingered wingtips.

PACIFIC BAZA - Very distinctive *crest, large yellow eyes*, grey face and throat, and *bold cross-bands on the chest and abdomen.* Broad rounded wings and long squarish tail with a black tip. Only found in north-eastern Australia, and across the top to the Kimberley. **Pages 18-19.**

black kite

BLACK KITE - The *long forked tail which is twisted and turned in flight* is the key feature. Dark blackish-brown above and below. The long wings have deep fingers. Usually congregate in flocks around dead animals, bushfires and cattle stations. Wheeling flocks are often seen high in the sky. Mainly found in northern Australia. **Pages 20-21.**

BRAHMINY KITE - More solid in the body and with shorter and broader wings than the black kite. The longish tail is square. The *head, neck and upper breast is white contrasting with the dark brown back, wings and abdomen.* Found along the northern coastline, where it scavenges along beaches and sometimes plunges for fish. Often seen perched around harbours and ports. **Pages 22-23.**

WHISTLING KITE - A pale streaked brown kite with deep fingers and slightly *downswept wings and long rounded tail.* Very buoyant flight and prominent calls. Adults have a dark rectangle along the trailing edge of the wing. Frequently seen at carrion and around lakes and swamps throughout Australia. **Pages 24-25.**

whistling kite

SQUARE-TAILED KITE - The *longish wings with deep fingers are held fairly high. The long tail is square. Glides slowly without flapping* over low shrubland and open forest in search of food. Mainly found in southern and eastern parts of Australia. **Pages 26-27.**

BLACK-BREASTED BUZZARD - *Soars high with broad upswept wings. Head and breast black with white patch in dark wing tips. Short rounded tail. Juveniles are mottled brown.* Mainly found in inland parts of northern and central Australia. **Pages 28-29.**

LITTLE EAGLE - *Solid looking eagle with very flat-held wings, with slightly upturned tips and a short square tail. Feathered legs* when seen perched. Several colour forms. *Pale diagonal bar across underwing* is obvious in flight. Soars with few wing flaps. Hunts by dropping on prey such as rabbits. Also feeds on carrion. **Pages 30-31.**

spotted harrier

SPOTTED HARRIER - *Flies low over grasslands and plains, with long high-held wings and no flapping.* Undersurface bright chestnut with white spots. *Prominent fingers on wings* and long slightly pointed tail. **Pages 32-33.**

SWAMP HARRIER - *Flies low over swamps, grasslands and farmlands with long high-held wings and no flapping.* Brown with *distinctive white rump.* Mainly found in wetter parts of eastern and southern Australia, being common in Victoria and Tasmania. **Pages 34-35.**

TYPICAL HUNTING HAWKS

These hawks have long, usually yellow, legs and toes, bright yellow eyes, short rounded wings and long tails. All are fierce hunters of small birds and sometimes small mammals. Males are much smaller than females. Some species are hard to tell apart and key features such as the length and tip of the tail (square, rounded or notched) are essential field characteristics.

BROWN GOSHAWK - Greyish-brown or grey above. The pale undersurface has fine reddish-brown cross-bars in the adults and bold vertical stripes in the juveniles. *The long tail is rounded.* Found throughout Australia and often around towns and farms. A fierce hunter, plunging into foliage when hunting birds. **Pages 36-37.**

brown goshawk

COLLARED SPARROWHAWK - Looks similar to the brown goshawk, but the *long tail is squarer and has a slight notch in the centre.* The female is the same size as the male brown goshawk but the male is much smaller. Found in the same areas as the brown goshawk but hunts differently, usually chasing its prey over longer distances. **Pages 38-39.**

GREY GOSHAWK - Two colour phases: either *pure white above and below; or grey above and white below* with fine bars. Found from the Kimberley, across northern Australia and down eastern Australia to Tasmania and Adelaide. **Pages 40-41.**

RED GOSHAWK - Larger than the brown goshawk with a *red head, breast and thighs.* The head has black stripes and the throat is pale. The wing tips appear dark in flight. The *longish tail has dark bands.* Flight is a series of quick flaps and glides and it is a swift hunter of birds. Found only in northern and eastern Australia. **Pages 42-43.**

SMALL KITES

Small, white-looking kites with small beaks, black marks on the long pointed wings, and long slightly notched tails. Usually seen perched or hovering.

BLACK-SHOULDERED KITE - Very pale grey above and *white below with a black shoulder patch, which is visible under the wing when flying.* Hovers into the wind like nankeen kestrels, but with more flapping and usually with dangling legs. Fairly fast flight, with alternate flapping and gliding with wings held high. Found throughout Australia, but most common in farmland and coastal parts of southern and eastern Australia. **Pages 44-45.**

LETTER-WINGED KITE - Similar to the black-shouldered kite when perched, but the *black extends in a line from the shoulder of the wing to the body when flying.* Mainly found in grasslands with few trees in inland Queensland and the Northern Territory, rarely moving to other parts of Australia. Sleeps in trees in the daytime and hunts at dusk. Sometimes in flocks of up to 50 birds. **Pages 46-47.**

letter-winged kite

FALCONS AND KESTRELS

Small to medium-sized with long, pointed and distinctively "elbow-angled" wings. Long tails. Some are very fast fliers and stoop on flying prey. Others hover and drop vertically on prey on the ground.

GREY FALCON - *Pale smoky grey on back,* with fine streaks on head and wings. *Wing tips dark.* The *undersurface appears white* but has fine vertical streaks. Juveniles are darker. Pale individuals of other species are often mistaken for this rarely recorded species. Found in drier parts of inland and northern Australia. **Pages 48-49.**

BROWN FALCON - This *heavily built, slow-flying falcon is* often seen perched on dead trees or poles, and is easily approachable. Has distinctive *dark moustache in pale cheeks.* Extremely variable in colour from dark brown to pale brown above and ranging from dark brown to almost white with dark stripes below. Generally, paler birds are found in drier inland parts of Australia. Usually in open country. Gives a *loud cackle when flying.* Catches food on the ground. **Pages 50-51.**

BLACK FALCON - A *large, black-looking falcon* with *broad wings* and a *long tail,* which is often fanned in flight, rather like a peregrine falcon. Found mainly in inland and northern Australia, but is rare. Many dark-coloured brown falcons are misidentified as this species. **Pages 52-53.**

PEREGRINE FALCON - A powerful-looking falcon with *black head and cheeks* and a *white bib.* Bluish-grey above and pale whitish below with fine bars on lower breast. Fast-soaring with fanned tail and a series of fast flapping and glides. Powerful shoulder-like flapping when chasing prey, and plummets with closed wings at incredible speed. **Pages 54-55.**

Australian hobby

AUSTRALIAN HOBBY - *Small falcon with darkish crown and face and a pale throat and collar.* The back is dark and the undersurface is rich brown. Fast flight low above the tree tops. Chases birds with fast powerful flight. **Pages 56-57.**

NANKEEN KESTREL - *A small pale falcon, usually seen perched* on a pole or tree or *hovering over grassland or low scrub.* Noticeably *white undersurface* with fine vertical streaks only seen when close by, dark wingtips and pale brownish back. The *tail has a black band,* which is more visible in the male. The habit of hovering motionless into the wind before dropping to the ground is an obvious identification cue which is shared only by the black-shouldered kite. **Pages 58-59.**

OSPREY
(Pandion haliaetus)

The huge nests of the osprey can be used by generation after generation and often reach up to two metres high. These massive domes of sticks and driftwood are usually lined with seaweed. Early seafarers thought they must have been built by a bird the size of an Andean condor. Although it is often incorrectly referred to as a sea eagle, the osprey is in fact a hawk.

DESCRIPTION: Mature adults are between 50 and 63 centimetres long and have a wing span of one and a half metres. The creamy white head is sometimes flecked with brown markings and a dark brown stripe runs on either side of the bright yellow eye to the neck. The underparts and legs are also creamy white, while the upper parts and upper wings are mottled light brown, dark brown and black. The bill is black and hooked.

OTHER NAMES: Fish hawk.

STATUS AND DISTRIBUTION: Ospreys live around most of the Australian coast. In northern Australia, ospreys are quite common and they are moderately common in the South-West, but the species has declined in South Australia and no longer breeds in Tasmania, Victoria and New South Wales. This decline may be due to pollutants causing breeding failures and deaths, and less habitat because of removal of large nest trees.

PREFERRED HABITAT: They frequent offshore islands and coastal areas, and in the Kimberley also move inland up rivers and on lakes.

LIFE HISTORY: Fish are the staple diet of ospreys. In the north they breed between April and July, and progressively later in the south. Clutch size is three, rarely four, eggs. Aerial displays during courtship are quite spectacular. The male hunts while the female incubates, broods and feeds the voracious chicks. The youngsters leave the nest about eight weeks after hatching.

CALL: Ospreys typically produce a short, quavering whistle.

WHITE-BELLIED SEA-EAGLE
(Haliaeetus leucogaster)

White-bellied sea-eagles can be seen on high vantage points near water or swooping on fish or other prey, their powerful wings uplifted. They land on the ground to tear their prey apart with their large talons. Tortoises, waterbirds, rabbits and carrion supplement the diet of fish. In the Kimberley these graceful creatures can be seen as far inland as Geikie Gorge, on the Fitzroy River, and Lake Argyle.

DESCRIPTION: Female white-bellied sea-eagles reach up to 84 centimetres long, whereas males are smaller with a maximum length of 76 centimetres. The head, neck, breast and underparts are snowy white in colour, sometimes with extremely thin, inconspicuous grey streaks. The back, wings and tail are almost black. The tail, however, has a broad white tip.

OTHER NAMES: White-breasted sea-eagle.

STATUS AND DISTRIBUTION: The species ranges around the entire Australian coastline and inland along rivers and lakes in good seasons.

PREFERRED HABITAT: This bird favours sea shores and islands, following large rivers and lakes inland. In fact it inhabits most places where there is extensive water. In the Kimberley, Northern Territory and Queensland, it can sometimes be seen near colonies of fruit bats, on which it preys.

LIFE HISTORY: Sea-eagles build enormous nests, up to four metres high, often perched high on a cliff. Breeding is between May and October. Two eggs are laid, several days apart, but the first-born monopolises all the food and the second usually dies. The female spends the most time sitting on the eggs and brooding, only relieved for short periods by her mate. She feeds the nestlings with food captured by the father.

CALL: The raucous cank-cank-cank resembles that of a goose.

15

WEDGE-TAILED EAGLE

(Aquila audax)

The wedge-tailed eagle is awe-inspiring, with its huge size, powerful wings and hooked bill. This majestic bird has a massive wing span of up to two metres. One of the most-maligned birds of prey, it was persecuted for decades because of the mistaken belief that it destroyed livestock. Australia's largest bird of prey now enjoys full protection. The birds are usually seen soaring over paddocks and woodlands in country areas.

DESCRIPTION: Wedge-tailed eagles have large legs and feet with deadly talons. Adult birds are blackish-brown to nearly black, while juveniles are a pale brown with creamy buff highlights. Seen from below, the tail is long and distinctively wedge-shaped.

OTHER NAMES: Eaglehawk, wedgie.

STATUS AND DISTRIBUTION: Wedge-tailed eagles are still moderately common and found in all parts of Australia.

PREFERRED HABITAT: These birds inhabit forests, open country and mountain ranges. They frequently feed on road kills and, as a result, they are often killed on country highways.

LIFE HISTORY: Depending on the landscape, the species nests in a variety of sites: in a low dead tree in a desert, a prominent tree top on a hillside, on the ground on an island, but always far away from human habitation. The nest is a large platform of sticks. There are normally two eggs but often only one chick survives. Immature eagles move out of breeders' territories, some moving to the coastal plains where they are often surprised in groups, squabbling over road kills. They hunt rabbits, small kangaroos and wallabies, and sometimes birds and reptiles.

CALL: These birds may make a variety of calls, such as a cat-like screech or repeated double whistle.

17

PACIFIC BAZA
(Aviceda subcristata)

The Pacific baza is a handsome bird which spends most of its time hunting in the tree tops. Stick insects are a favourite food, but frogs, reptiles and insect larvae are also snatched from leaves. Their slow, easy wing beats allow them to weave through tree crowns or perform acrobatic feats, occasionally even snapping up insects on the wing. They have also been observed crashing into trees to disturb prey.

DESCRIPTION: These birds have piercing yellow eyes, greyish-brown and cream bars across their belly and a rufous suffusion around the legs and beneath the tail. The broad, dark bluish-grey wings are quite rounded. Adult males are distinguished by a black crest. The birds are between 35 and 43 centimetres long.

OTHER NAMES: Crested hawk, Pacific lizard-hawk.

STATUS AND DISTRIBUTION: In WA, Pacific bazas are found only in the Kimberley region. They also inhabit the northern part of the Northern Territory and a broad band down the eastern seaboard to south of Sydney. Elsewhere, they are found in a number of Pacific islands, including New Guinea and the Solomon Islands.

PREFERRED HABITAT: Pacific bazas often patrol the edges of eucalypt forests and especially riverine woodlands. They are frequently seen in gardens and orchards near the eastern coast of Queensland.

LIFE HISTORY: The female usually lays two or three eggs in a rather small nest at least 15 metres above the ground. Both parents co-operate to build the nest and incubate the eggs, which takes just over a month. Other parenting duties, including food collection, are also shared.

CALL: During courtship and nest building, the Pacific baza emits a whee-choo. A variety of calls are given at other times.

BLACK KITE
(Milvus migrans)

Black kites are scavenging birds often seen around towns, especially near rubbish tips. They usually forage in flocks, or perch together in trees, seeking respite from the heat. Twenty to 30 of these birds will often follow fires spreading through savannah grassland, circling and dropping through the smoke in search of an easy meal.

DESCRIPTION: These large birds grow up to 55 centimetres long. They are predominantly dark brown, with a lighter brown head and neck, wing patches and underparts. The flight feathers are quite black and the dark brown tail has black bars. The tail has a shallow fork and it twists and turns in flight.

OTHER NAMES: Fork-tailed kite, Kimberley seagull.

DISTRIBUTION: These birds are common throughout most of the Australian mainland, being absent only from south-western WA and a section of the eastern coast. They are also found in Europe, north Africa, southern Asia and New Guinea.

PREFERRED HABITAT: Black kites inhabit a range of habitats, including woodland and savannah areas, and can almost always be seen circling over towns in northern Australia.

LIFE HISTORY: Although the bulk of their diet is obtained from scavenging carrion and other scraps from the ground, black kites will sometimes swoop on live rodents, reptiles and insects, which may be swallowed in flight. They build a platform of sticks up to 30 metres above the ground on which to lay two or three eggs which are incubated by the female. During nesting, the male obtains most of the food but does not directly feed the young. Black kites usually nest between March and May, but also nest from August to September.

CALL: The call of this bird is a quavering kwee-err or series of staccato whistles.

BRAHMINY KITE
(Haliaster indus)

The Brahman is a member of the highest Hindu caste and it is easy to imagine why this regal-looking and strikingly-coloured creature was given such a name. The Hindus regard it as sacred. These birds range all the way to India, southern China, and the Pacific, but their distribution in Australia is quite limited.

DESCRIPTION: Brahminy kites have a snowy white head and chest, a bone-coloured beak and reddish-brown back and wings. They are between 45 and 51 centimetres long. Females are larger than males. As well as their distinctive colouring, they can be recognised by their square, short tails and almost perfectly horizontal wings during flight.

OTHER NAMES: Red-backed sea-eagle.

STATUS AND DISTRIBUTION: The brahminy kite occurs on offshore islands and coastal areas right around northern Australia, from Shark Bay in WA to the Hastings River in New South Wales.

PREFERRED HABITAT: They live in mangrove and mudflat areas, near beaches or along rocky shores, having their own territorial stretch along the coast.

LIFE HISTORY: In Australia, the brahminy kite feeds mainly on fish but will also take frogs, reptiles, insects and other animals, such as crabs. They generally breed during the northern dry season (April to October), building large stick nests. These are lined with seaweed, leaves and other material. Although one to three (usually two) eggs are laid, just one youngster generally survives to fledging, which takes up to 55 days. The female spends most of her time at the nest until the young kites are about three weeks old, then she will join her partner to hunt for food for them.

CALL: These birds usually call only when breeding, typically making a keee-e-yeh or a meowing sound.

23

WHISTLING KITE
(Haliaster sphenurus)

The whistling kite's loud, whistling call is the main reason for its name. It is graceful in flight, whether gliding, soaring or flapping, when its long-fingered wings and long, rounded tails are noticeable. When gliding, its otherwise horizontal wings are held downward at the tip. It has a similar appearance to the little eagle.

DESCRIPTION: The buff-coloured head and neck grades into a mid-brown back and wings and deep brown flight feathers. The underparts are creamy and buff, with some streaking, and the tail is a light greyish-brown. The birds are 50 to 55 centimetres long, with the females being slightly larger.

OTHER NAMES: Carrion hawk, whistling eagle.

STATUS AND DISTRIBUTION: Whistling kites inhabit most of Australia and a number of Pacific islands.

PREFERRED HABITAT: The most favoured areas are open woodlands near water. You are unlikely to see them in dense forests, in deserts with few trees, or near built up areas.

LIFE HISTORY: Unlike most other raptors, it is possible to see whistling kites in groups. They may gather around carrion such as road kills, but the birds also hunt alone for small animals such as birds, mammals, reptiles, fish and invertebrates. More than one pair may even nest in the same tree. The female incubates two or three eggs in a large, leaf-lined nest of sticks. The male hunts for the family for the six weeks that the young take to fledge.

CALL: These noisy birds call with a long shrill whistle, followed by a number of short, rapidly ascending notes.

Below: *Feeding on a dead brolga*

SQUARE-TAILED KITE
(Lophoictinia isura)

Small birds, reptiles and insects, plucked from the tree tops, are the main quarries of the square-tailed kite. The nestlings of honeyeaters are a particular favourite. The square, light grey tail tipped with black and dull whitish windows near the tip of the wings will help you to recognise these birds. Despite being known as a kite, this bird is thought to be most closely related to the black-breasted buzzard.

DESCRIPTION: The face of the square-tailed kite is quite white, with a yellow eye, while the upper body is a mottled brownish-black. All underparts are rufous brown, streaked with black. The birds are about 50 to 56 centimetres long and, like most raptors, the females are largest.

STATUS AND DISTRIBUTION: Square-tailed kites range across most of the Australian mainland, but are absent from the central and northern deserts, from the Nullarbor Plain and from built up areas in the eastern states.

PREFERRED HABITAT: The square-tailed kite is very much a bird of the trees. Woodlands and open eucalypt forests are its usual haunts.

LIFE HISTORY: Two or three eggs are laid in a large nest, up to one metre in diameter, in the bough of a eucalypt high above the ground. The female does most of the nest building, incubation and chick rearing, with some help from the male. The male is the main food provider.

CALL: Though usually silent, square-tailed kites sometimes make a quick quavering call or a yelp.

BLACK-BREASTED BUZZARD
(*Hamirostra melanosternon*)

Despite their name, black-breasted buzzards do not always have a black breast. The breast, throat and upper belly may also be pale reddish-brown with black streaks. They prefer all kinds of live prey, from birds to grasshoppers, rabbits and small wallabies, and usually treat carrion with disdain. These birds will shamelessly rob the nests of other raptors and feed the young to their chicks. Like many other raptors, buzzards engage in spectacular aerial displays during courtship.

DESCRIPTION: The head, back and wings of the black-breasted buzzard are dusky black, with rufous highlights. The lower belly and undertail is reddish-brown. The birds are 55 to 60 centimetres long. Seen from below, the black-breasted buzzard has a short, square tail. Its long, upswept wings are rounded at the tips and there are large, white, round markings at the base of the flight feathers.

OTHER NAMES: Black-breasted kite.

STATUS AND DISTRIBUTION: These birds are well established in northern and central Australia. They are generally missing from southern Australia, Tasmania and most of the eastern seaboard.

PREFERRED HABITAT: Black-breasted buzzards nest in eucalypt-lined watercourses in deserts and other arid areas.

LIFE HISTORY: They construct the nest on a large stick platform in the fork of a tree, in which they deposit one to four (usually two) eggs, laid several days apart. The young take about six weeks to fledge but the first born takes most of the food and is usually the only one to survive. Both parents take turns to nest, hunt, and feed themselves before passing scraps to the young. After fledging, the young remain dependant on their parents for several months.

CALL: The call is a rapidly repeated two or three syllable cry.

A captive black-breasted buzzard attempting to break an egg.

LITTLE EAGLE

(Hieraaetus morphnoides)

The little eagle is an attractive bird. Birds of the lighter colour phase are a quite beautiful mixture of dark brown, light brown and russet, with white-feathered underparts. The little eagle has a stouter build and a shorter, squarer tail with broader, more rounded wings, upturned at the tip, than the similar whistling kite. It sometimes makes use of thermals to spiral upwards to great heights.

DESCRIPTION: The little eagle has both a light and a less common dark colour phase. Lighter birds have a greyish-brown tail with dark brown barring that is nearly white at the tip. Darker phase eagles are almost a uniform dark brown. The underparts are either whitish (in light phase birds) or dark brown (in dark phase birds), but the feathers always cover the feet, right down to the toes. Males are about 48 centimetres long and females are about 55 centimetres in length.

STATUS AND DISTRIBUTION: The species inhabits most of mainland Australia, and is absent only from arid areas that include the Goldfields and the treeless Nullarbor, as well as parts of the Northern Territory and the tip of Queensland's Cape York Peninsula.

PREFERRED HABITAT: Little eagles have a definite preference for wooded areas.

LIFE HISTORY: Young rabbits provide the bulk of the little eagle's diet. The relatively small nest is usually placed high in a tree. Though one to three eggs are laid, usually only one chick will survive to fledge, taking about 60 days to do so.

CALL: Little eagles typically deliver a soft whistling call of two or three syllables, with the last two syllables shorter and lower in pitch. A variety of other sounds are also sometimes made.

SPOTTED HARRIER

(Circus assimilis)

Spotted harriers generally inhabit dry, open plains and shrubby areas. They search systematically for food, criss-crossing their territory, usually within five metres of the ground. Prey is always obtained from the ground.

DESCRIPTION: The spotted harrier is a striking creature with an owl-like head and attractive white spots on its reddish-brown underparts. The legs are quite long for a raptor, and lanky. Males are about 53 centimetres long and females average 60 centimetres long.

OTHER NAMES: Allied harrier, Jardine's harrier.

STATUS AND DISTRIBUTION: Swamp harriers are found across most of Australia, but are missing from a few coastal and far northern and southern areas, especially those places which are heavily forested.

PREFERRED HABITAT: Inland areas are preferred, especially dry, open plains and shrublands. They are sparsely distributed and quite nomadic, due to the boom and bust cycle of many of the arid areas they inhabit.

LIFE HISTORY: When they are not breeding, swamp harriers are generally solitary birds. Building a new nest every year, usually between July and October, spotted harriers lay two to four eggs. The eggs take just over a month to incubate. The resultant chicks have a definite pecking order, which can affect survival in times of scarcity.

CALL: A rapid kit-kit-kit-kit is made when the birds become alarmed.

SWAMP HARRIER

(Circus approximans)

Their powerful hooked beak and piercing yellow eye gives the swamp harrier an authoritative appearance. Watch for them gliding over wet pasture and marshy areas, with long upswept wings, with the aim of surprising waterbirds, small mammals, frogs, reptiles and large insects. Its long black talons are adept at plucking such prey from reedy undergrowth.

DESCRIPTION: Swamp harriers are a mottled dark brown, with a much lighter coloured greyish-brown tail and creamy buff underparts. The females are browner in colour and larger. A whitish band is evident on the lower rump when they fly overhead. Adults are 50 to 58 centimetres long.

OTHER NAMES: Marsh harrier, Gould's harrier, swamp hawk.

STATUS AND DISTRIBUTION: In WA, swamp harriers are distributed across the south-western corner, from Shark Bay to Israelite Bay, and in a band across the central Kimberley. They are found in most of the rest of Australia, apart from the most arid zones and in New Zealand and southern New Guinea.

PREFERRED HABITAT: Swamps, wet pastures and inland river systems.

LIFE HISTORY: Swamp harriers hunt, feed, roost and nest near the ground. Spectacular courtship manoeuvres, however, take place in the air, sometimes involving more than one pair. The nest is a stick and grass platform, usually concealed in reeds or rushes over water. Three to six eggs are laid and most young survive to fledge after about six weeks, unless killed by older chicks if food is in short supply. The male transfers food to the female in mid-air near the nest.

CALL: Swamp harriers are birds of few calls and generally silent. While courting, however, they emit a whistled kee-a and have a psee-uh food call during breeding.

BROWN GOSHAWK

(Accipiter fasciatus)

Brown goshawks prey on a variety of birds, mammals, frogs and reptiles, usually taking them completely by surprise. Their liking for the young of domestic "chooks" has earned them the name of "chickenhawk".

DESCRIPTION: Females are larger than males; they are between 47 and 56 centimetres long, compared with the 40 to 43 centimetre males (though northern forms of this species are considerably smaller). The wings and back of this bird are deep brown, with a more rufous collar. The tail is brown, with darker brown barring, and the breast and underparts are beautifully patterned with chestnut and cream barring, which must offer these stealth hunters superb camouflage. The eyes are a piercing yellow.

OTHER NAMES: Chickenhawk, Australian goshawk.

STATUS AND DISTRIBUTION: Brown goshawks range across most of Australia, with the exception of a few central areas, and extend to Tasmania, New Guinea and other Pacific islands.

PREFERRED HABITAT: They are common in eucalypt forests and woodlands, and along inland watercourses lined with trees, avoiding areas with no cover. They are also well represented in urban areas.

LIFE HISTORY: Both partners build their nest of sticks with great care, taking up to four weeks to do so. The nest is large and placed in the horizontal fork of a tree, high off the ground. The female does most of the incubation, after laying from one to five eggs at intervals of between two and four days, while the male brings food to the nest for mother and chicks.

CALL: Brown goshawks are usually silent, but do make a variety of sounds when excited or disturbed.

Photo – Babs & Bert Wells/CALM

COLLARED SPARROWHAWK
(Accipiter cirrhocephalus)

The collared sparrowhawk will occasionally visit gardens when hunting small birds. It sometimes kills caged birds such as canaries and budgerigars.

DESCRIPTION: This medium-sized hawk is extremely difficult to distinguish from the brown goshawk. Goshawks, however, have long and rounded tails compared with the long, square tails of sparrowhawks. The males of both species are much smaller than the females. Goshawks are larger than sparrowhawks and the female is accordingly quite large. Male goshawks are the same size as female sparrowhawks, while the male sparrowhawk is quite small. Adults of both species are grey or brown above and the undersurface is pale, with a beautiful cross-barring of pale chestnut. Juveniles are dark brown above and the underside has vertical brown streaks. The beak, eyes and legs are yellow, while the wings are rounded.

STATUS AND DISTRIBUTION: Collared sparrowhawks are found throughout Australia and on islands to the north, such as New Guinea.

PREFERRED HABITAT: These birds inhabit forest and woodlands, especially in areas with many small birds.

LIFE HISTORY: The open, bowl-shaped nest is made of sticks, usually lined with green leaves, and placed in a tall tree. The same nest is used for several years and increases in size each year. Two or three eggs are usually laid and are white with pale brown markings. Incubation and fledging each last about five weeks.

CALL: A loud kik kik kik is made by the birds, usually while perched. They are mainly silent in the non-breeding season.

GREY GOSHAWK

(Accipiter novaehollandiae)

Small birds, mammals up to rabbit-size, reptiles and insects are the favoured food of this lightning-fast predator. It attacks ferociously and persistently, regardless of whether the prey is in the air or on the ground. Grey goshawks have a long, rounded tail and broadly rounded wings.

DESCRIPTION: In north-western Australia, grey goshawks are usually completely white, with a black beak, reddish-brown eye and yellow legs. However, as the name indicates, there is also a grey colour phase, with bluish-grey flight feathers, white underparts and a lighter grey head and breast. The neck and breast usually features fine white barring. Grey goshawks vary between 34 and 54 centimetres long, and the female is markedly larger than the male.

OTHER NAMES: White goshawk, grey-backed goshawk.

STATUS AND DISTRIBUTION: In WA, the grey goshawk is confined to the Kimberley region, from Derby northward. It is also found in northern areas of the Northern Territory and Queensland around the eastern seaboard and in Victoria and Tasmania, to near Adelaide and on Kangaroo Island in South Australia. It also extends to New Guinea and islands in the Pacific.

PREFERRED HABITAT: The bird inhabits timbered areas within reasonable distance of the coast, including pockets of Kimberley rainforest.

LIFE HISTORY: Grey goshawks breed between April and January, but earlier in the north than the south. Two to four eggs are laid in a solid stick nest high up in a tree. Nest building is a shared activity, but the female spends the most time sitting on the eggs. The male brings food to the nest for the female to feed to their young, which fledge in about five to seven weeks.

CALL: A variety of calls are made while the birds are breeding, otherwise they are silent.

RED GOSHAWK

(Erythrotriorchis radiatus)

Red goshawks are rare and secretive birds, found largely in northern and eastern Australia. In WA they are listed as threatened. They are stealth hunters, swooping mainly on other birds, generally at dusk and dawn. Most of their hunting is done in the tree canopy, and they will also take mammals and large insects if the opportunity presents itself.

DESCRIPTION: The flight feathers and tail are mottled with reddish-brown, black and white. The head, neck and breast are lighter in colour but heavily streaked with blackish-brown. The thighs and undertail are a light russet colour. Red goshawks are 45 to 58 centimetres long.

STATUS AND DISTRIBUTION: Red goshawks are quite rare. They are found from Derby in WA's Kimberley region, to the Hunter River in New South Wales, occupying a broad coastal and subcoastal band.

PREFERRED HABITAT: In these areas they inhabit tall woodlands and riverine vegetation, and also live around the edges of rainforest.

LIFE HISTORY: Red goshawks are believed to occupy a large territory. The female constructs a nest of sticks and twigs in the fork of a tree at least seven metres from the ground. She also sits on the eggs and cares for the young, while the male brings food for the family. The young take about seven or eight weeks to fledge.

CALL: They make a repeated skeep when alarmed.

BLACK-SHOULDERED KITE
(Elanus axillaris)

Black-shouldered kites spend the day hunting rodents, reptiles, frogs and insects. They can often be seen hovering in the air, somewhat more laboriously than the nankeen kestrel, before plunging to the ground to snatch their victims with powerful talons. You are more likely to see them gliding, with upstretched wings, in the early morning or late afternoon.

DESCRIPTION: These magpie-sized birds have a distinctive black patch on the shoulder of their wings. Otherwise, their upper bodies are pearly grey, with darker grey primary wing feathers. The head and neck are snowy white, with a black beak. They are white beneath, with a small black spot under each wing. The white tail is square in shape. In flight, the dark-tipped wings, although broader than those of the nankeen kestrel, can look quite pointed.

STATUS AND DISTRIBUTION: They are reasonably common and found throughout most of Australia.

PREFERRED HABITAT: Black-shouldered kites live mostly in woodlands, grasslands and especially farmland.

LIFE HISTORY: Courting black-shouldered kites soar and flutter together and may lock claws in mid-air. The female, which is slightly larger, then carries the dangling male down. Each pair builds a new cup-shaped stick nest every year between April and October, and raises three or four young. The male's job is to hunt, while the female broods. The young fledge in about five weeks. They feed on mammals, lizards and large insects. Like all birds of prey, they regurgitate pellets of undigested bones, fur and skins, which may reveal the source of their last meal.

CALL: Black-shouldered kites call with a rapid, whistling chip-chip-chip and make a wheezing noise in defence.

LETTER-WINGED KITE

(Elanus scriptus)

The letter-winged kite is Australia's only semi-nocturnal raptor. It is also the only species that lives in true colonies. The mainstay of its diet are the rodents that may reach plague proportions in the deserts following good rains. The long-haired rat is a particularly important food species. The most striking characteristic of this attractive and graceful bird is the black marking on the underside of the wings, which looks like an M or a W, depending on the position of the wings.

DESCRIPTION: This bird has quite large, black-ringed eyes that give its face a somewhat owl-like appearance. Its upper parts are white merging into grey, while its underparts are white.

STATUS AND DISTRIBUTION: Letter-winged kites are generally rare, but may be quite abundant in good seasons. They breed in an area extending through interior parts of the Northern Territory, Queensland, South Australia and New South Wales, but are quite nomadic according to seasonal conditions. In 1997, for instance, a number of birds were recorded in WA, as far afield as Port Hedland and Broome. At the time, rains were poor in their usual haunts and there were good rains on the west coast.

PREFERRED HABITAT: Open plains with clumps of trees are their favoured habitat, but they will move to coastal areas when food is scarce.

LIFE HISTORY: Letter-winged kites usually breed in colonies of between two and 100 pairs. The female is the primary nest tender, while the male is the food bringer. In good seasons, the female may lay again in another nest before the young fledge, leaving the male to care for them. However, despite the high rate of reproduction at such times, there will be a high rate of mortality when conditions return to normal.

CALL: The species communicates with other birds with a harsh karr and emits a kik kik kik when alarmed.

GREY FALCON
(Falco hypoleucos)

The grey falcon is one of Australia's most uncommon and rarely seen raptors and in WA it is listed as a threatened species. The birds are usually seen along eucalypt-lined rivers and streams in the arid interior, where they will perch on a branch to watch for a likely meal. On spying a small mammal, insect, reptile or bird they will strike with terrific speed, snatching the hapless creature from the ground or in mid-air.

DESCRIPTION: The upper body of the grey falcon is grey, with indistinct black streaks. The face and underparts are a slightly paler shade of grey. In flight its darker grey, barred tail is fanned out. It also has a yellow eye ring, fully feathered legs and yellow feet. Males are about 34 centimetres long and females average 43 centimetres in length.

STATUS AND DISTRIBUTION: The grey falcon ranges from WA's Pilbara and Kimberley regions in a broad swathe across Australia's central deserts, inhabiting most of South Australia and inland Queensland, New South Wales and Victoria, but is completely absent from the eastern coast and from Tasmania. It may be quite nomadic in poor seasons.

PREFERRED HABITAT: They mainly inhabit plains with few trees.

LIFE HISTORY: Two to four (usually three) eggs are laid in the old nest of another bird. The female does the bulk of the incubation, relying on her mate to find food. As the young become older she will spend more time hunting away from the nest. They take about six weeks to fledge but usually remain with their parents for several months before striking out on their own.

CALL: When agitated, the grey falcon makes a rapidly repeated kek.

BROWN FALCON
(Falco berigora)

The brown falcon may glide, in search of prey, with its wings held in a shallow V. However, its favourite method of hunting is to perch on a high vantage point until it detects movement. Then it will suddenly swoop down to snatch the rodent, rabbit, small bird, lizard, snake or large invertebrate that will provide its next meal.

DESCRIPTION: The colour of this species varies from almost black to rufous above and cream below. There is invariably, however, a dark tear-shaped mark below the dark brown eye. All colour forms also have dark brown flight feathers with buff spots or bars and a greyish-brown, barred tail. Males are about 45 centimetres while females average 50 centimetres.

OTHER NAMES: Brown hawk, cackling hawk.

STATUS AND DISTRIBUTION: The brown falcon is reasonably common in all parts of Australia and is found in New Guinea and other Pacific islands.

PREFERRED HABITAT: It usually inhabits open grassy woodlands or forests, agricultural areas and towns.

LIFE HISTORY: Rather than building its own nest, the brown falcon usually lays two to five eggs in the old nest of another hawk. The mother spends about a month incubating the eggs. The father shares some nesting duties but spends most of his time searching for food. The young fledge after 40 days or so.

CALL: Its loud calls, especially while breeding, have earnt this species the name cackling hawk.

BLACK FALCON

(Falco subniger)

Large birds, such as ducks, and other warm-blooded prey, such as small rabbits or rats, are the favoured food of the black falcon. This raptor is an agile bird that often snatches its unsuspecting victims in mid-air. It is nomadic, patrolling the open sparsely treed country of the interior during good seasons and moving to more coastal areas in poor ones.

DESCRIPTION: Black falcons are distinguished by having dark sooty brown plumage, however the underside of the pointed wings has some white barring. There are also some white markings on the face. Males average 45 centimetres long, while females are 55 centimetres in length.

STATUS AND DISTRIBUTION: The black falcon is mainly an eastern Australian species, living predominantly in inland Queensland, New South Wales, South Australia and the Northern Territory. It disperses to coastal areas and the northern part of WA during times of drought and food shortage.

PREFERRED HABITAT: Black falcons like open habitats, with fewer trees, near water.

LIFE HISTORY: Breeding between June and December, they reuse the nest of another large bird. Two to four eggs are laid. The females spend the bulk of the time at the nest, while the males provide food for the family. The young take about six weeks to fledge, but the mother will usually continue to feed them for many more weeks.

CALL: Black falcons may make a moaning karrrrr or a repetitive gak-ak-ak.

PEREGRINE FALCON
(Falco peregrinus)

Peregrine falcons are known for their incredible speed. They can swoop at speeds of up to 300 kilometres per hour, leaving prey little chance of escaping. Their main victims are racing pigeons, and other birds up to their own size, and even sometimes larger than the falcons themselves. On capture peregrine falcons will pluck their prey, then take it to a quiet place to consume. The name *peregrinus* means wanderer and refers to the migratory habits of birds in the northern hemisphere.

DESCRIPTION: The throat, breast, underwing and other underparts of the peregrine falcon are a creamy buff colour, with fine black barring below the breast. The head, wings and back are dusky. Males average 38 centimetres and females 48 centimetres long.

OTHER NAMES: Black-cheeked falcon.

STATUS AND DISTRIBUTION: They are found in all parts of Australia, but are common nowhere and are classed as being in need of special protection. These deadly predators are found in all continents, being distributed throughout Eurasia, Africa and North and South America.

PREFERRED HABITAT: Peregrine falcons can be seen on cliffs, along rivers, and even in tall city buildings.

LIFE HISTORY: The peregrine falcon will occupy an area of between 20 and 50 square kilometres, returning year after year to the same nest site. Rather than build a nest, it will lay two to four eggs in an alcove within a cliff, in the hollow of a large tree or in the old nest of another bird. The female does most of the incubation, which takes about a month, while the male obtains most of the food. The young fledge in about five or six weeks.

CALL: The birds scream repeatedly when alarmed, make short, sharp calls in flight and shriek during courtship.

AUSTRALIAN HOBBY

(Falco longipennis)

The Australian hobby will chase down and kill other birds, sometimes larger than itself, or dive on them from above. When hunting at dusk, bats and large flying insects may also be killed by this method.

DESCRIPTION: The sides of the face around the dark brown eye, and sometimes the crown, are dusky, while the rest of the head is buff coloured. Males are about 30 centimetres long and females are generally 34 to 35 centimetres long.

OTHER NAMES: Little falcon, white-fronted falcon.

STATUS AND DISTRIBUTION: The Australian hobby is distributed through all parts of Australia, except for a small area in south-western Tasmania. It is relatively common in wooded areas. In winter it heads to warmer climes in the north, and some birds migrate to New Guinea and surrounding islands.

PREFERRED HABITAT: Open woodlands are the preferred habitat, and the birds will visit urban parks.

LIFE HISTORY: The Australian hobby lays two to four eggs in the nest of another bird. Once a pair has taken up residence, they will defend their adopted nest with vigour. The female sits on the eggs for about a month, briefly leaving the nest to accept food from the male. Two or three young will usually fledge in approximately five weeks.

CALL: The Australian hobby has a shrill and repeated call.

NANKEEN KESTREL
(Falco cenchroides)

The nankeen kestrel is usually seen over grassy areas, where it sits quietly on power poles or on the very tips of tall trees, looking around in search of insects, lizards and small rodents. It often gracefully hovers head to wind, with head downturned, looking for prey. When it spies a likely meal, the bird drops like a stone to impale its prey on razor sharp talons, then alights on a pole or fence post to dismember the food.

DESCRIPTION: These handsome, but relatively small, birds of prey are about 32 centimetres long. They have a bright rufous brown back and creamy white underparts, with thin black streaks on the breast. The tail has a black bar near the tip and is grey in the male and barred in the female. The legs are yellow, and there is a black patch below the eye.

OTHER NAMES: Australian kestrel.

STATUS AND DISTRIBUTION: The species is common and found throughout Australia.

PREFERRED HABITAT: This bird is most common in open woodland and agricultural land, where it can easily see prey on the ground.

LIFE HISTORY: Kestrels are a common sight over open grassy country and low vegetation. Along the coast, many pairs nest in niches in limestone cliffs, either on the mainland or on offshore islands. Inland, the birds lay their eggs in tree hollows, on buildings or on cliff faces. Like all falcons, they never build their own nest but may reuse the old nests of other birds. The four or five eggs are whitish, with blotches of reddish-brown, and are incubated by the female.

CALL: A high-pitched, repeated ki or harsh twitter.

59

CARING FOR INJURED RAPTORS

If you find an injured bird of prey or any other native animal, the following steps should be taken:

1. Using a towel or jumper, carefully pick up the injured bird or animal. Be gentle but firm, and very careful of sharp claws, strong beaks and powerful legs. Place the animal on a towel in a cardboard box that is big enough for it to stand upright or lie flat. Do not wrap or constrict birds, as this causes great stress which can result in death. Close the lid of the box and secure with tape. Call an animal rehabilitation centre for assistance if you are unable to catch the animal.

2. Do not feed or give water to any animal you rescue. Incorrect diet combined with stress often causes death. An animal that appears friendly, quiet or calm is often in shock and will die quickly if not correctly treated.

3. If you are unable to bring the animal immediately to a raptor rehabilitation centre, place it (in its box) in a quiet, warm place to help reduce its stress levels. Avoid checking the animal, as your friendly and concerned face may seem threatening and will cause stress levels to rise again. Please refrain from retaining the animal any longer than necessary as this will reduce its chances of survival.

4. Call a raptor rehabilitation centre immediately, as the sooner the animal receives professional care, the better its chances of survival and release. All animals that are capable of surviving are returned to the wild.

Photo – Courtesty of Raptor Retreat

Katie McCreadie from the Raptor Retreat with a wedge-tailed eagle

SIGHTING RECORD

SPECIES	REMARKS
osprey	
white-bellied sea-eagle	
wedge-tailed eagle	
Pacific baza	
black kite	
brahminy kite	
whistling kite	
square-tailed kite	
black-breasted buzzard	
little eagle	
spotted harrier	
swamp harrier	

Osprey

SIGHTING RECORD

SPECIES	REMARKS
brown goshawk	
collared sparrowhawk	
grey goshawk	
red goshawk	
black-shouldered kite	
letter-winged kite	
grey falcon	
brown falcon	
black falcon	
peregrine falcon	
Australian hobby	
nankeen kestrel	

Photos – Babs & Bert Wells/CALM

Osprey chicks

INDEX

4343-0298-10M